wealthy LIFE SKILLS

Praises for *Wealthy Life Skills*

"WEALTHY LIFE SKILLS, is a great book for anyone who want to unleash their potential to be successful! The book can also be an eye-opener, that everyone has the ability to become whoever they want to be!"

—**Dr. Henry L. Causly,**
Henry Causly Ministries, Inc.

"Wealthy Life Skills truly caters to people who want to change their lives for the better. I love how it inspires people to live the life they have been dreaming of. It is truly a must read!"

—**David L. Hancock**,
Founder Morgan James Publishing
Chairman, Guerrilla Marketing International
President, Habitat for Humanity
Peninsula & Greater Williamsburg

"Wealthy Life Skills" contains simplified, easy-to-follow, step-by-step, wealth-building strategies. This incredibly phenomenal book shows how anyone, in any walk of life, can set and achieve wealthy goals."

—**Beverly Washington**,
Federal Government Department of Defense
Environmental Engineer

"I am at a loss for words to express how your, *Wealthy Life Skills* book has awakened my lifelong dream of revealing the potential in people to live out the plan God has purposed for their lives! This book gives simple, reasonable steps to accomplishing each goal to succeed. These simple steps take away the FEAR of getting started on your journey to success.

I recommend this book to those who are still dreaming, yet waiting to move towards those dreams becoming a reality."

—Ollie U. Litt
Evangelist, Educator, Coach
Zama Japan

"*Wealthy Life Skills* is an amazing book that's easy to understand while teaching people that they have what it takes to succeed and achieve financial abundance."

—Dr. Steve K. Branch
Multi Million Dollar Earner
Coaching, Training and building Teams U.S.A.

"*Wealthy Life Skills* is one book that truly caters to people who want to change their lives for the better. I enjoy my free time reading good books and articles.

This is one among the best books that caters to most people. Its a must read! God Bless"

—John & Vinolia Clayton, India

"*Wealthy Life Skills* is an empowering book that simplifies the process of gaining wealth. This easy to read book breaks down and corrects the misconceptions about finances and teaches you to incorporate life skills en route to financial success. A must read for the young and older age group."

—Demetrius Kilgore,U.S.A

wealthy
LIFE
SKILLS

*Gaining Wealth
Using Your Own
Skills and Abilities*

Veronica M. Brooks

NEW YORK

wealthy LIFE SKILLS
Gaining Wealth Using Your Own Skills and Abilities

Published in New York, New York, by Morgan James Publishing. Morgan James and The Entrepreneurial Publisher are trademarks of Morgan James, LLC.
www.MorganJamesPublishing.com

The Morgan James Speakers Group can bring authors to your live event. For more information or to book an event visit The Morgan James Speakers Group at www.TheMorganJamesSpeakersGroup.com.

A FREE eBook edition is available
with the purchase of this print book

CLEARLY PRINT YOUR NAME IN THE BOX ABOVE

Instructions to claim your free eBook edition:
1. Download the BitLit app for Android or iOS
2. Write your name in UPPER CASE in the box
3. Use the BitLit app to submit a photo
4. Download your eBook to any device

ISBN 978-1-63047-168-2 paperback
ISBN 978-1-63047-169-9 eBook
ISBN 978-1-63047-170-5 hardcover
Library of Congress Control Number:
2014933888

Cover Design by:
Rachel Lopez
www.r2cdesign.com

Interior Design by:
Bonnie Bushman
bonnie@caboodlegraphics.com

In an effort to support local communities, raise awareness and funds, Morgan James Publishing donates a percentage of all book sales for the life of each book to Habitat for Humanity Peninsula and Greater Williamsburg.

Get involved today, visit
www.MorganJamesBuilds.com.

Habitat
for Humanity®
Peninsula and
Greater Williamsburg
Building Partner

Table of Contents

Foreword

The first words that should be uttered on the pages of this book are simply this "Congratulations."

Congratulations to you, the reader, for having the smarts (and the guts) to open this particular book for a read. You deserve validation already because many wouldn't even see its worth (as they are blind to self betterment) or be willing to confront its message (there is WORK to be done if you're to succeed). So, well done on pushing through those initial barriers and discovering the help Veronica Brooks offers within these pages. You're in for a treat.

Congratulations as well to Veronica, whom I consider a friend and a peer in our quest to help others find their purpose, their power and their success so they can live in happiness. To scour through all the false hope messages and find the precise tidbits of truth out there is like finding a needle in a haystack. But she's done exactly that, here, for us.

There is such a wealth of information (on wealth) in this book that I'd like to make a suggestion on how to get the most out of it. A friend and mentor of mine once posed the question about digesting a ton of information "How would you eat an elephant?" to which the is simply "One bite at a time." So, take-in this plethora of content one paragraph, one page, one chapter at a time. I found it best to just read through it cover to cover and enjoy it once; then returned for a second time through, taking notes along the way of all the realizations and exciting new ideas it conjured up for me. However you read it, enjoy and USE the advice to better yourself, your business, your life – you deserve it.

To your brilliant success!

David Lee Jensen, #1 Bestselling Author,
Fortune 500 Speaker, Inc. 500 Coach
www.DavidLeeJensen.com

Acknowledgement

First of all, I would like to thank Reava Nurse. Thank you for your great wisdom, support and inspiration. You inspired me to believe that I can live my dreams and be whoever I want to be. Also, I am grateful that you accompanied me on the live Radio Show in San Antonio, TX. I just want to tell you that you were awesome!

To Les Brown, I want to express my gratitude for being a mentor to me for the last two decades. Through you, I have learned to "LIVE FULL AND DIE EMPTY" that "IT IS NOT OVER UNTIL YOU WIN!" and to "SHOOT FOR THE MOON BECAUSE EVEN IF YOU MISSED, YOU'LL LAND AMONG THE

STARS". Thank you for believing in me and pushing me forward to greater heights in life. To me, you will always be my Papa Motivator and Life Mentor.

To Rick Frishman, founder of Author 101 University, I want to thank you for inspiring me to write a proposal for Morgan James Publishing and for inviting me to attend Author 101. I really did not know what to expect, but I just went for it and I am so glad that I did. It was a great honor to be selected from over 7,500 people to work with Morgan James Publishing.

To W. Terry Whalin, Acquisitions Editor Morgan James Publishing, I can still clearly remember that just when I thought I had missed the opportunity to turn in my proposal, you stopped me in the lobby. You asked me one simple question: Did you get a chance to submit your book proposal? I said no because I was too busy talking to everyone else. You said let's sit down so that I can give you a short pitch about my book proposal. I am glad you stopped me in the lobby. Thank you for your desire to inspire people to succeed into becoming bestselling authors.

To Brandon Burchard, thank you for highly motivating me to succeed. I will always remember what you said to me, and that is, to keep moving forward. That is one life lesson that I will forever carry with me.

To my loving husband, Glen E. Brooks, thank you for always encouraging me to move forward in life. Thank you for the greatest gifts that you gave to me, our three loving sons Joe, Eugene and Quintail. You all inspire me to reach for my dreams.

Last, but definitely not the least, THANK YOU TO ALL OF YOU. Thank you for believing that I can help and inspire you to have a successful, happy and contented life.

Chapter 1

THE PREPARATION

EVERYTHING YOU NEED TO KNOW ABOUT GOAL-SETTING

Why Are Goals Essential?

Have you ever wondered why some people are successful in everything that they do, while others seem to be the total opposite? If you think that you are destined to be part of the "average group", then think again. All you need is to reassess your goals in life to help you get back on track. If you want to be successful in life, what you need to do is to understand how to accomplish things. The first step is to determine your goals that will be the driving force of your actions toward accomplishing the dreams that you have.

The problem comes in when you do not know what you really want. Even if some people seem to think that they know what they want, in reality, they don't. When deciding what you really want to do, the desire should come from the heart. If you want to become a winner, you have to understand what path you want to take.

In doing this, you need to know first where you are at the moment. From there, you will know what steps you need to take to arrive to where you want to go. This concept is the same with using a map. In order to reach the destination, you need to first know your location. This is one valuable life lesson.

By setting your goals, traversing in life will be easier. If you have goals, you will always be reminded that no matter what problems come your way, your destination will always be there waiting for you. This destination is the fulfillment of your dreams.

Without goals, it will be like traversing in a dark alley without light. Your goals will be your guide while you are passing the dark alley called life.

One of the most important lessons you need to remember is that **goal setting is your ticket to transform your life from an average one to a great one.**

Without your goals, you will not have direction when it comes to what path you really want to take.

Once you have achieved your goals, you will be able to feel a sense of fulfillment that will guide you to do greater things.

Take Action

Set Your Goals

Live a Satisfying and Successful Life

Golden Rules When It Comes To Goal Setting

1. **When setting your goals, you need to remember to make your goals SMART:**

Specific

Measureable

Attainable

Relevant

Time-bound

Specific

When setting your goals, they should be specific. In addition, it should be clear and not generalized. Your goals should be well defined so that you know what parameters you need to include. The vagueness of goals may lead to confusion.

Measurable

It is also important that your goals are measurable. This means that the degree of your success can be defined after you have done all the steps to attain your goals. For example, your goal is to reduce unwanted weight. How will you know that you are successful in your goal to lose weight?

You may set your goal as this:

After 3 months, I should have lost 15 pounds of excess weight by following a healthy diet and regular exercise.

As you can see, you can clearly measure your goal by stating that you should lose 15 pounds. If you lost 15 pounds after three months then you are successful.

Attainable

It is important that the goals that you have set for yourself are attainable. If you have set goals that are too impossible, then you will just demoralize yourself including your confidence.

For example, you want to lose weight; you came up with a goal to lose 20 pounds in 1 week. Do you think this is possible? It is definitely not possible to lose 20 pounds in 1 week unless you are trying to kill yourself.

However, this does not mean that you should only settle for easy to attain goals. Goals that are too easy will not be able to test your abilities and discipline. If you can, you should always challenge yourself.

Relevant

When setting your goals, you should keep in mind the direction that you want your life to take. This will help you set goals that are relevant for your future.

Time-Bound

If you want your goals to be achieved, you need to set a deadline to your goals. Setting a deadline will also improve your focus on your tasks.

2. Your goals should always motivate you.

If the goals you have set motivate you it will be easier to focus on what you want to achieve. Through motivation, you will be pushed harder especially in times when you want to give up.

3. Write your goals.

If you do not put your goals into writing, you may not remember all the goals that you have set for yourself.

Writing all of your plans will help you have a clearer view of what you want. This will help you in fulfilling everything that you want

You can try a TO DO list to know what goals you need to accomplish first.

A TO DO list can help you prioritize the things that you need to accomplish. Moreover, it can also help you focus even more.

4. Do not forget the importance of action plans.
If you do not have action plans, it is impossible to attain your goals. Your action plans include everything that you will do in order to achieve the goals you have listed.

To put it simply, your action plans represent every step that you have to fulfill your dreams. Without an action plan, your dreams will remain as they are...only dreams.

For example, if you want to lose weight, your action plan may include the following:

- Decrease your carbohydrates during meals
- Run for 15 minutes every morning
- Eat healthy foods

*IMPORTANT NOTE: Write the visions, dreams and goals down. Make it plain and simple that in all your getting you will have a clear understanding of what you want to accomplish in life. *

PLAN TO SUCCEED

ARM YOURSELF WITH LIFE SKILLS

The Life Skills That You Need To Know)

If you want to be wealthy, you need to equip yourself with skills that can help you in life. These skills are called life skills. To help you understand this even more, I will be explaining to you an important acronym that can change your life for the better.

The acronym I want you to remember is none other than **LIFE SKILLS**.

L stands for learning

Life itself is a learning process. If you want to succeed and become wealthy, you need to continually learn different life lessons. Four aspects of learning include critical thinking, creative thinking, communication and collaboration. Critical thinking is a focused, careful analysis of something to understand it better. Creative thinking is an expansive, open-ended invention and discovery of possibilities. Communication is the process of transferring a thought from one mind to others and, in return, receiving thoughts back. Collaboration is working together with others to achieve a common goal. These are interpersonal skills that must be learned in order to function within society properly.

I stands for identifying yourself

Identifying yourself means having self-awareness. It also means having confidence in your skills and abilities. If you will not believe in yourself, who will?

Self-awareness is an essential toward maximizing your management skills and are considered to be basic life skills. Have confidence in yourself and your abilities. Know who you are, and where you stand at this point in your life. Then look to where you want to be, in say 10 or 20 years from now. As long as you can understand and use your abilities, you will accomplish what you want in life.

F stands for being fit

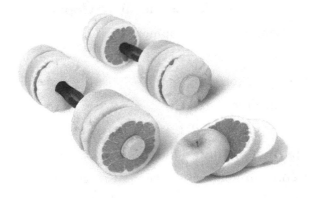

In order to face the challenges that life may bring, you need to be fit and healthy. Your health should always be part of your top priorities. With good health, you can achieve anything that you want to reach.

Staying fit and healthy is a very important aspect of life skills. Your health should be one of the most important things in your life. Cooking is one of the most basic of life skills that must be mastered in order to take care of your family. If you serve your family under cooked food, you might end up making them sick. Daily exercise is also another very important basic life skill that will take care of you for life. Hygiene is also very important as it directly affects your health. Keeping fit and healthy in your life will allow you to achieve the goals that you have set for yourself.

E stands for emotional development

Your emotional development includes your ability to interact with other people. Expressing yourself properly in society is one of the skills that you need to learn. Emotional development is a very important interpersonal life skill that takes years to master, for the majority of us. This is the basis of who we are and how we communicate with others. We have to learn very early on how to communicate with others, as it directly affects the outcomes of many different situations. For instance, say that you are attending your first dance and you are so shy, that you appear to others to be arrogant. If you cannot express your feelings properly, you may have a hard time in dealing with these types of situations. If you learn how to express yourself properly in society, you will find many rewarding experiences in your lifetime.

S stands for solving problems

Life will bring you different challenges. Because of this, it is important that you know how to solve your problems. It is a very important coping skill that may determine whether you will succeed or not. Decision making and coping skills are very important interpersonal skills that must also be learned in order to operate successfully within society. Coping skills involve the ability to make decisions and the ability to handle success and failure during different situations. We make decisions on a daily basis, from what time to wake up to what time we go to sleep, and everything in between. Making good decisions is essential to accomplishing your short and long term goals. So, make sure that you are capable of making good decisions and coping with success and failure

K stands for kindness

Kindness is an important value that is inherent in everyone. If you know how to give kindness, other people will bring back the goodness to you also. Moreover, if you show kindness to other people, you can expect more blessings to come your way. According to Webster's dictionary, kindness means one of two things: a kind deed or a favor, or; the quality or state of being kind. In essence, this is another interpersonal skill that can be learned, but is usually inherent within us. Although most of us do learn this skill, some people do not ever learn this concept. This is an essential skill to have when dealing with people from different cultures or mentalities. Knowing how to be kind to others will ensure that you get your message across in the right way.

I stands for Intimacy

You should know how to become intimate with the people you love. It does not necessarily mean sexual intimacy. It may also be about caring, sincerity and thoughtfulness. Intimacy does not involve only a sexual interaction. There is so much more to intimacy including having a good relationship with working clients and other individuals. Although this does not sound like intimacy, it is in fact a form of intimacy. When you deal with anyone in your life, you are having an intimate moment. Whether it is telling a customer service agent that you are not interested, to telling your husband that you love him, they are each in their own way, an intimate moment in life.

L stands for living a balanced life

We all need to know how to balance the different facets of our lives. Without balance, our life may be chaotic and difficult. Stress management is another very important aspect of interpersonal skills, which are necessary for daily life. Knowing when to move to action and when to relax is an essential skill, which will ensure that you accomplish the goals that you have set for yourself. Everything must always be in balance, overall, in your personal and work life, in order to succeed with your goals. Exercise, such as

Yoga, can be very beneficial in teaching you control, balance, strength and relaxation in all of your personal and work activities.

L stands for letting go

In order to be happy, we need to learn to let go. Letting go does not only refer to people and things, it can also mean letting go of negative emotions and thoughts. Why does it seem that we cannot let certain things go in life? Because we are afraid to get out of the driver's seat and let the universe take control. This seems like a very simple concept, but is one of the hardest to actually accomplish for most of us. But this is a very important concept to master if you want to operate in today's society properly. Letting go, trust and faith all rely on our ability to believe that despite what we can see with our eyes, there is a lot more going on in what we cannot see.

S stands for social skills

Without the right social skills, you cannot be wealthy and abundant in life. Remember, no man is an island. We all need company and companionship. Social skills are important in every aspect of our lives. From the time that we are small children to the time that we go to a nursing home we use social skills. Social skills are imperative in order to operate within society.

Once you grab hold of these life skills and take action in using them to enhance your life you will be on your way to achieving your dreams and goals.

MAKE YOUR SUCCESS REACHABLE: STEPS TO YOUR SUCCESS

Now, I will teach you specific ways to succeed.

FIRST: Optimism is good, but it can also propel you into false security. Pessimism can be helpful as an initial predicament in any situation. However, this should never run your life. Believe that you can achieve great things, just do not fall into complacency.

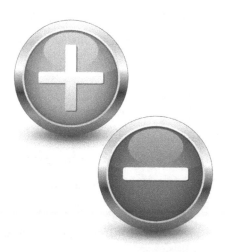

SECOND: Consider self-control, self-awareness and self-discipline as very important. By doing, you will be able to develop faith in yourself. Moreover, you will be able to appreciate your innate, inherent and latent qualities.

Always listen to the voice within you and remember that you have a DYNAMIC WILLPOWER.

THIRD: Learn to live beyond the demands of the mind. This is important to be able to embrace the road to wealth. You can do this through constant vigilance, self-analysis, introspection and understanding.

To put this simply, you need to learn that there is no such thing as a free lunch. In order to attain success, you need to work hard for it.

To make everything easier, what you should do is to find what makes you happy. From there, find out if it is possible to make a living from doing what you love. Also, remember that if you do not start, you will not succeed. This is very true especially if you want to gain wealth and success. If you will not move, wealth will not come to you.

Dreams don't work unless you do

FOURTH: Have a strategy. Without a strategy, you are like a soldier coming to war without ammunitions. If you want to gain wealth, you need to know what you will do to make everything happen.

FIFTH: Once you have achieved your goals and gained the wealth that you want, you need to share it with others. By sharing, you will be able to appreciate more the very essence of life.

THE LAW OF PROSPERITY

We all want to prosper. We all want to achieve success, abundance and great wealth. Because of this, we all need to know the law of prosperity. This law will guide our every step in reaching our dreams.

If you are wondering, what the law is about, it is actually very simple. It all comes down to **selflessness and contentment.**

It is not bad to desire success and all the good things that life can offer, but when this desire is not doing you any good, it can be **dangerous.**

To affirm your abundance, you need contentment. Any selfish desire can lead to failure.

This is a **very powerful spiritual law** that we need to follow.

In your daily life, you should:

- ALWAYS BE GOOD TO EVERYONE AROUND YOU
- DO NOT BE TREACHEROUS AND DECEITFUL
- BEWARE OF EGO
- ALWAYS BE TRUE AND SINCERE
- HELP OTHER PEOPLE AS MUCH AS POSSIBLE

- MEDITATE DAILY AND VISUALIZE YOUR SUCCESS
- REASSESS YOUR GOALS
- ALWAYS HAVE A SENSE OF GRATITUDE

The true way to being wealthy is by following and living all the good virtues instilled in us. This is our real and true nature as human beings. If all of the good virtues are practiced by everyone, the world will surely prosper even more.

USEFUL TIPS TO BECOME FEARLESS

If you want to gain wealth, it is important to become fearless. When I say fearless, I am not just talking about eliminating all your fears. Fear is normal so there is no way to totally eradicate this feeling.

What I am trying to say is that you should be fearless when it comes to conquering the things that are hindering your success. These things block your way in achieving the dreams that you have.

Now, I will be listing for you some useful tips to become fearless.

1. Be aware of what you fear. By doing so, you will be able to know how to conquer it.

2. Always remind yourself of this known fact:

**80% of fears and worries
NEVER HAPPEN**

3. Share your fears. Share what you feel. By doing so, you will not be so preoccupied with the fears that you have.

4. Read and get motivation to conquer your fears from good books. There are a lot of reading material that can help you win over your fears.

5. Visualize good things as much as possible. This is vital to help you appreciate the beauty of being fearless.

6. Do not forget to put things into perspective. Drive all the negative thoughts away.

POSITIVE THINKING

HAPPIER YOU

OVERCOMING FEAR OF FAILURE

"Shoot for the moon. Even if you miss, you'll land among the stars."

-Les Brown

If you want to succeed and gain wealth, you need to be brave enough to rise above your fears. Only those who confront their fears are able to achieve the goals that have set for themselves. If you are not brave enough, you will not be able to reach your full potential.

To overcome your fear, you can do the following:

1. **DO SOMETHING ABOUT IT**

   You should not let fear immobilize you. If you do not try, you will surely fail. In case you fail, you will be able to create awareness of the factors that will contribute towards your success.

2. **FIND ALTERNATIVES**

   Try doing things differently to help you overcome your fears. Try alternatives to achieve your goals if you do not succeed. Remember, you should never associate yourself with failure.

3. **LEARN FROM FAILURE**

To overcome your fear, you need to learn how to appreciate the lessons that you learned from the failures that you have experienced. When you failed in your endeavors, take it as a learning experience. Reassess where you have gone wrong and do not be afraid to try again.

"Success is not final, failure is not fatal;
it is the courage to continue that counts."
                                    -Winston Churchill

Chapter 2

THE
ACTIONS

WAYS TO UNLOCK WEALTH

If you want to unlock wealth, then this is your lucky day! Today, I will be teaching you the most important principles when it comes to unlocking your wealth and abundance that you want to achieve in life.

What you need to realize is the opportunities to unlock wealth is waiting for you. If you feel that there is no more chance for you to live a comfortable life, you are wrong. You have what it takes to be wealthy. All you need is to know how to unlock your possibility for greatness.

Before tackling the principles that you need to know, it is first important to understand that:

Wealth Is More Than Just About Money. It Is Also About Success And Abundance.

The principles that I will be listing here are all centered on our innate qualities. These principles also have a spiritual basis that can amazingly work to your advantage to make wealth, abundance and success flow into your life.

The principles are the following:

- Truth
- Righteousness
- Peace
- Love
- Non-violence

If you learn to incorporate these principles/virtues into your life, you will surely succeed in the different facets of your life. This I can say, without any doubt.

The reason is quite simple.

You will not go wrong with these principles because they are the lessons of our codes of conduct and moral values.

They are the very law of nature. If you obey the law of nature, your pursuit of wealth will always be on track.

ON TIME AND MONEY: THE TYPES OF PEOPLE IN THE WORLD

There are four types of people in the world:

1. People with no time, no money
    People under this type are mostly employees. They have no time because they are working for long hours, but still their money is not enough.
2. People with no time, lots of money
    People under this type are the professionals and small business owners. They usually earn more than other regular employees.
3. People with time and no money
    People under this type are those with no source of stable incomes. They are unemployed or dropouts.

4. People with time and lots of money
   This is what most people want to achieve. You can only do so if you learn how to use your money.

Where do you belong?
REMINDER: Do not work for money.
Let your money work for you.

IMPORTANCE OF TIME MANAGEMENT

How to Manage Your Time Well

TIME IS LIMITED,
YOU NEED TO USE IT WELL

Successful people know how to use their time well. If you have problems when it comes to managing your time, you can follow the tips I will be listing here just for you:

- First of all, you need to know how to prioritize. Important tasks may be given more time if needed.
- Do not fall to time wasters. Time wasters are activities that are not that important, but can take a lot of your time. An example of this is daydreaming. Instead of daydreaming, you should wake up and start the tasks at hand. Another example is watching the television too much.
- Do not delay doing things. If you delay the tasks that you have, there is a tendency that you will not finish anything. As much as possible, you also need to set deadlines.
- Start early so that you will be more fruitful. Did you know that early risers are more productive? In fact, it is more healthy because sleeping in can make you more prone to health problems such as headache, depression and obesity.

REMEMBER: TIME IS PRECIOUS

CHECKLIST: WHAT YOU SHOULD ASK YOURSELF WHEN IT COMES TO MANAGING YOUR TIME

- What are my priorities?
- Am I happy with the way I manage my time?
- Do I use my time well to reach my goals?
- Am I motivated with the way I manage my time?
- Is my schedule balanced?
- Do I have time for all the important people in my life?
- Is my time efficiently used everyday?
- Do I need to manage my time better?

- Does my schedule reflect the things that I want to achieve?

A CLOSER LOOK ON HOW TO GAIN WEALTH

Basic Steps to Gain Wealth

To help you on your quest to gain wealth, here are some valuable guidelines that you may follow to pave a wonderful path to your ultimate success. The guidelines are simple and easy to follow.

1. Determine what you are good at and start from there. It is also imperative to do what you love.
2. Set your goals and work to achieve them.
3. Always be motivated and do not stop learning.
4. Be persistent and do not let failure hinder you to try again.

5. Be innovative. Use creativity to gain the results that you want.

6. Invest not only money, but more importantly time and effort.

   You do not need to be a millionaire. Start with what you have and let your investment grow.

7. Learn to manage your time effectively. **WEALTHY PEOPLE KNOW HOW TO VALUE TIME.**

8. Always give back. Help other people especially if you have achieved already the desires of your heart.

ATTRACTING WEALTH AND MONEY

Money Talk: Steps To Personal Wealth

We all want to become rich and financially abundant. If you are still working your way up to financial independence, do not worry or fret. It may be a difficult and long journey, but you will reach your goals if you know what to do.

To gain personal wealth, you may follow the following tips and guidelines:

- **HAVE THE DESIRE TO ACHIEVE YOUR GOALS.**

- **HANDLE MONEY EFFICIENTLY. KNOW HOW TO BUDGET WELL AND KNOW YOUR NEEDS VS WANTS.**

This is where discipline comes in. Even if there are many temptations to spend your money, you need to learn how to weigh your needs and wants.

- **DO NOT SPEND MORE THAN YOU EARN.**

If you spend more than you earn, you will never have enough savings. The best thing you can do is to determine the amount of money you will save each time you get your paycheck.

- **STAY FOCUS.**

- **INVEST YOUR MONEY WISELY. PLAY SMART AND KNOW YOUR PRIORITIES.**

3 WAYS OF MAKING MONEY

These are three ways to earn money:

- **Trade your time for money**- This is what employees and the self-employed do.
- **Use your creativity to earn money**- This is for the investors and artists. If you have the ability and skills, you can always use it to earn the money that you need.
- **Use the resources that are available**- People can earn money with the resources that you have included manpower. This is what business people and leaders do.

The question now is, how do you want to achieve your wealth?

ANSWER: IT IS STILL YOUR CHOICE

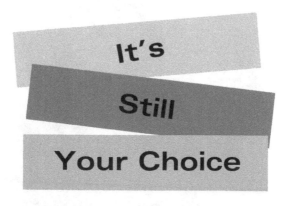

USING YOUR ABILITIES AND SKILLS TO GAIN THE WEALTH THAT YOU WANT

Abilities And Skills: Your Ladder To Succeed

If you want to gain wealth, you need to start with the resources that you have. These are not just about your financial resources, it also includes your abilities and skills.

To put it simply, play with your strengths. For example, if you are good in baking, you may start selling your baked goods to your families and friends. This can be a start. Your business may start small, but it has the potential to become an empire if you know how to handle it.

AGAIN, PLAY TO YOUR STRENGTHS.
USE YOUR ABILITIES AND SKILLS.

START A BUSINESS IN 4 EASY STEPS

One of the best ways to gain wealth is to start your own business. If you think that it is a complicated process, you are wrong. You can actually start a business in four easy steps. Today, I will be sharing with you a secret to start a business no matter how much capital you have.

STEP 1: OPEN UP AND INVESTIGATE—You should use your abilities, skills, ideas and talents to explore ideas for a business. Do not rush in choosing. If you want to succeed, exert time and effort to find the best business venture that you can take.

STEP 2: ESTABLISH WHAT IS OF GREAT VALUE—In this step, weigh the advantages of the business that you want to start. Ask yourself this question: How will this help people?

STEP 3: CREATE A SYSTEM FOR YOUR BUSINESS—Be creative in creating a business system. Let your business work for you and not the other way around.

STEP 4: BEGIN SELLING—Word of mouth is your best way to advertise. Make sure that your products are good so more people will be enticed to buy your products.

IMPORTANCE OF BUSINESS ETHICS

In order to be successful in your business, you need to adhere with good business ethics.

Business ethics refer to the behaviors that a business adheres to when it come to their dealings with clients and vendors.

Our ethics serves as a guide whether our actions are right or wrong. They are also important when it comes to decision making.

Some important values that you should use not only in your business dealings, but in everyday life as well include the following:

HONESTY

If you want customers to trust you, it is important that you should show them that you are honest with all your business dealings.

INTEGRITY

Aside from honesty, integrity also includes the values of accuracy and stability.

RESPONSIBILITY

For you to be successful in life, you need to know how to be responsible for your actions and decisions. This is especially important in businesses. If you have a business, there is no time to pass the blame when things go wrong.

QUALITY

Without quality, your business will not last for a long time. One of the most important considerations of customers/buyers is the quality they can get from a company/business establishment.

RESPECT

The respect I am talking about is not just the respect that you give to your customers. It also includes the respect you should show your employees and co-workers.

Moreover, in order to succeed in your business, you should respect all the laws that the society has set.

LEADERSHIP

As a business-owner or manager, you need to live by example. You need to become a good leader so that people will follow you.

TEAMWORK

It is important to learn to value teamwork. What you need to remember is that you cannot achieve all the work alone. You will need other people to help you achieve your dreams and goals.

TRUST
To put this simply, you need to learn to trust and be trustworthy as well.

Examples of Unethical Business Practices That You Should Avoid

- Giving out misleading information about your products and services
- Inappropriate marketing tactics
- Bullying employees
- Not following safety precautions in your business establishment.

KNOW HOW TO INVEST

When you hear the word investment, what comes to your mind? Most people will probably think of money, banks and even stocks. These are all correct, but what you need to understand is that investing is not just about money, stocks and companies.

Today, I will be talking about the most important investment that you will take away. I am talking about **INVESTING IN YOURSELF**.

Yes, you have read it right, investing in yourself is very important if you want to gain wealth. Your parents invested in you by sending you to school, but this is not enough. After going to school, you can invest in yourself by continuously learning especially in the financial aspects of your life.

How can you do this?

Invest in your ***Financial IQ.***

Your financial IQ is not just about having money. It is about developing a healthy relationship with money and building a wealth of assets that can help you generate more wealth.

If you have a high financial IQ, you will surely have an easier time when it comes to choosing what is best for you in different situations. It will be your armor during stressful times.

IMPROVING YOUR FINANCIAL IQ

In order to gain wealth using your skills and abilities, you need to improve your financial IQ. To do this, just follow the tips listed below.

Be organized. Always keep track of your expenses and income. You should always track the flow of your money.

Know how to budget your finances. As much as possible, only buy your wants if you know that you have saved enough.

When investing, invest in assets that have increased long-term values. If something brings you more income, it is an asset. Do not invest too much on liabilities such as cars.

Always think ahead. Do not just live in the present. Thinking about the future will help you focus more on your goals.

How to Get Out of a Financial Mess

If you are currently having troubles financially, you do not need to worry too much. There is still a way out. All you need is to know what to do. There are two strategies that you may try to get out of the financial mess that is ruining your chances of a wealthy and abundant life.

DEFENSIVE STRATEGY

In this strategy, you need to cut down your spending. Starting a business is not a very good idea if you are already in a financial mess. Remember, cash flow is more important than revenue. Also, do not buy anything that can be considered a liability. Your thinking should be: What can I invest in today that will give me funds tomorrow?

OFFENSIVE STRATEGY

If you have great business skills, think of a low-cost way to invest. For example, you can join a network marketing company or you can just start your own online business. If you use this strategy, you should not be afraid to take risks.

Whatever you want to follow, it is up to you. Weigh the pros and cons of your situation to come up with the best solution to your financial problems.

Chapter 3

THE DESTINATION

AFFIRMATIONS

In order to be truly wealthy, affirming yourself is very important. Every morning, you can read these affirmations to help you go through your day:

- I am blessed.
- I am beautiful.
- I will be wealthy.
- There is always hope.
- There is no reason to give up.
- My faith is bigger than my problems.
- I will be successful.

- There is nothing that can stop me from reaching my dreams.

FINANCIAL ABUNDANCE

We all want to gain wealth. The good news is **WE ALL CAN**.

There is nothing that can hinder you from achieving the things that you want to reach if you just have the right attitude and life skills. **Today, you may not be in the place where you want to be financially, but do not worry, with hard work and dedication; you will surely arrive at your destination.**

I hope that you will be able to use all the lessons that you have learned today to create yourself and your family a **better and brighter future**.

Just always remember the principles because they will guide you on your journey.

Again, you can gain wealth and abundance. Just know your destination.

The destination I am talking about is **FINANCIAL ABUNDANCE AND SUCCESS**.

I believe you can reach your dreams.

I believe in you.

I wish you a fruitful, abundant and beautiful life.
AGAIN, ANYTHING IS POSSIBLE.
Love,
Veronica M. Brooks

About the Author

Veronica M. Brooks was born and raised in Albuquerque, NM. Although, she considers Jacksonville, Florida as her home station after living there for over 20 years. She completed an Associate Arts Degree in Political Science from Florida State College, a Bachelors Degree in Business Administration, and a Dual Masters Degree in Business Administration Management and Human Resource Management. Back in 2000, she was appointed in the Department of Defense. Presently, she is serving as the Supervisory Contracting Officer at Naval Air Facility, Atsugi, Japan.

Her previous assignments include:

- The Fleet Industrial Supply Command (FISC) Naval Regional Contracting Center in Manama, Bahrain which included contacts that are essential to meet Central Command (CENTCOM) requirements all throughout the Middle East, Southwest Asia, East Africa, the Indian subcontinent, and Department of Defense (DoD) activities in the United States
- Resident Officer in Charge of Construction (ROICC) and Integrated Product Team (IPT) at the Naval Air Station In Jacksonville, FL,
- Secretary for the Naval Air Depot in Jacksonville, FL
- The Department of Dependent Schools (DoDDs) Office Automation Assistant in Zama American High Schools located in Japan.

Veronica is Defense Acquisition Workforce Improvement Act (DAWIA) Level III certified. Being true to her calling, she is also an active member of the National Association of Professional Women,

JAX Chamber of Commerce, American Chamber of Commerce Japan, For Empowering Women Japan (FEW), National Contract Management Association (NCMA) and the African American Federal Executive Association (AAFEA). She is also the Voluntary Leader of non-profit organizations, which are geared towards mentoring women and their families.

Her personal decorations include:

- The Presidential/Congressional Recognition Award for Business Woman of the Year from 2006.
- She was published in the Wall Street Journal for Businesswomen of the year Award 2006.
- She was also published in the Wall Street Journal for the Outstanding Leadership Award of Business Advisory Council in November of 2006.
- Six Special Act Awards of outstanding performance in her position duties.

Veronica M. Brooks is an international speaker, motivator, mentor and coach. Her mission is to encourage and help people all over the world. As an accomplished writer, she wrote the book "Ninety

Days to Start Gaining Wealth". She is also the owner of Ministry Webmaster, a web designing and media advertising company. She provides information and resources to assist people in obtaining a healthy lifestyle, while creating wealth for the rest of their lives. It's not over until you win!

As for her hobbies, Veronica loves to spend quality time with her family. She also enjoys horseback riding, creating wealth, travelling across the globe and empowering people, especially women to be the best that they can be.

COME DREAM BELIEVE AND ACHEIVE
WITH VERONICA M. BROOKS AT
www.veronicabrooks.com
www.wealthylifeskills.com

INVITE VERONICA M BROOKS
TO COME SPEAK AT YOUR EVENTS
www.veronicabrooks.com

SIGN UP FOR YOUR DAILY DOSE AT
www.veronicabrooks.com

Also By Veronica M Brooks

Ninety Days to Start Gaining Wealth
Power of Integration Marketing

SEMINARS BY VERONICA M BROOKS
Wealthy Life Skills
Ninety Days to Start Gaining Wealth

WEBINARS BY VERONICA M BROOKS
Provides an Atmosphere of Achieving Your Dreams
    and Goals
Prepares Training in Networking, Life Skills, and
    Fearlessness
Provides Steps about Transformation of the Mind
Attitude to Believe Out the Norm
Transformed with a New Way of Thinking to Achieve
    Your Desired Goals
The Positive Atmosphere of Giving

BONUS PACK

90 DAY COACHING PROGRAM

Get one month FREE access to Veronica's 90 Day Coaching Program valued at $332.00 savings from the standard package price!

You will find in this package a lot of great strategic tools that will enhance your inner skills and abilities to maximize your profits. If you want to be successful in life, this coaching program is what you need.

To claim your FREE one month coaching, just visit us at www.gainingwealth.com. Enter your name and email, and in the comment section, insert this statement "Coaching Access by Choice" then click submit!

FREE 15 ACCESS TO LIVE CALLS WITH VERONICA BROOKS

This call could be a life changing experience for you!

All you have to do is to visit her website at www.wealthylifeskills.com to sign up. Once you have logged in as a member, just proceed to Veronica Brooks Access

Questionaire. At this point, you will have the chance to schedule your call with Veronica. Based on your questionnaire, Veronica will ensure your call is effective and straight to the point so you can get the best result.

FREE eBook
Power of Integration Marketing gives you the essential steps to create a win-win situation for you by helping you maximize your profits. Also, you will be able to learn what online business collaboration can do for your business and your promotion from being home-based.

"Integration internet marketing is the unification of marketing processes, sometimes called distribution channels, for a common or related purpose."

Visit Us at www.veronicabrooks.com, and insert promo code "BONUSWLSPOIM1022" during the purchase process to be able to download the free eBook.

CPSIA information can be obtained
at www.ICGtesting.com
Printed in the USA
JSHW020216230622
27371JS00003B/383

9 781630 471682